William Carey

'He died, but ... still speaks'

William Carey 1761-1834

Margaret G. Williams

The window was the gift of John Campling, village doctor from 1960 until his retirement in 1989. For many years he was a deacon at Carey Baptist Church, Moulton. It was designed and made by stained glass artist Paul Casciana and the pewterer Tom Neal, and was installed in 1995.

William Carey's time at Moulton brought many challenges to him and to others. Perhaps the most important is depicted in this stained glass roundel in the church porch. His conviction grew that:

* God's love encompassed the whole world
* as seen in the life, death and resurrection of Jesus
* as made known through the Bible
* which everyone needed
* in their own language

The Church was challenged to join in the Mission of God—to

Expect great things from God, and
Attempt great things for God.

Introduction

For a number of years I have been privileged to welcome visitors from all over the world to our church and cottage museum at Carey Baptist Church, Moulton. They have wanted to trace the early life of William Carey. Sometimes we have been a team welcoming them for a carefully planned visit; sometimes it has been the Minister, or someone else, but most often it has been my responsibility to respond to telephone calls requesting access to our cottage museum. (Our website states that visits are by appointment only, but many people arrive 'on spec', hoping to find it open: risky!) Sometimes it has been an individual, and occasionally several coachloads. Often people have also wanted to visit Paulerspury, Hackleton, and Kettering – all part of *The Carey Experience*. Olney and Central Baptist Church Leicester have also welcomed visitors. Some visitors may speak very little English and need a translator. Often this results in a great sense of connection with the world-wide Church and the Church throughout the ages. We have seen people weep with emotion and sink to their knees in fervent prayer. The story and the sense of place have great power to challenge today's Christian pilgrims, and even those who may not profess any Christian faith.

The story is of a weaver's son with few prospects, but who dreams dreams and achieves amazing things: the story of a boy with a very basic education who would found a university and become one of its first professors: the story of a country boy of humble birth who never loses his humility. As a pioneer, he faced many difficulties and needed much flexibility in making bold decisions. He was frequently out of his comfort zone, often misunderstood, sometimes making mistakes.

It is a story to inspire, but we don't tell it to glorify this man: he would hate that. It is a story of what God can do when a person is totally committed to doing his will. It's a story many visitors feel is their story too. In 1922 a plaque was put on the cottage where William and his wife Dorothy lived, which finishes with a quotation from Hebrews 11:4: 'He being dead yet speaketh'. It is obvious that the challenge he experienced, and the challenge of the story lives on. So at the end of each section there are questions for reflection and discussion. How does that challenge relate to our world today, especially to today's Church?

The approach is thematic, rather than simply biographical, so there is some repetition, but with additional detail. A great many books have built up a picture of William Carey's life and thought, and not all of them agree on details, but the one I return to over and over again is S. Pearce Carey's *William Carey*, especially the 8th edition. This is because, as his great grandson, the author did so much research both in Britain and India, and had access to a huge pool of written sources, not all of which have survived. He even met people whose parents had spoken to them of his great grandfather and colleagues. He visited Moulton as a guest speaker on the occasion of Centenary celebrations in 1934.

My hope in writing this is that Carey's challenge may be heard by a new generation as still relevant. The Church, society and the world are very different but the Great Commission of Matthew 28:19 is timeless. As Carey argued at a meeting of Northampton ministers, Jesus' command to his followers to share and demonstrate the good news of God's love for the whole world was accompanied by the promise to be with them to 'the end of the age'.

MGW 2023

Carey's Moulton Cottage next to the church

CONTENTS

The Challenges

1. The bigger picture

*'For God so loved **the world**...' John 3:16*

Imagine the scene: it is a summer day in 1761 and in a small cottage in Pury End, Paulerspury, in South Northamptonshire, Edmund Carey the weaver works hard at his loom. He is weaving tammy cloth to make outdoor clothing. It is time-consuming work and when finished it has to be taken and sold. His wife Elizabeth is expecting their first baby any day and is glad of the support of Edmund's mother, Ann, who lives with them. But on August 17th everything stops when a boy is born, to the delight of all three. He's named William after his grandmother's much loved son who died as a young man. What dreams did they have for this baby boy? Perhaps he would be a weaver like his father, or maybe even a teacher like the William who had died. He was taken to the village church to be baptised at the font just three days later. Grandmother hoped he would grow up to look after his parents just like they were caring for her. How astonished they would have been if they had known he would start a Christian mission movement that would change the world; that he would live most of his life in India, becoming a famous author, Bible translator, lexicographer and publisher; that he would become a social activist, a famous botanist, and much more.

St James' Church Paulerspury was to play an important part in his childhood. When William was just six years old, Edmund was delighted to be offered the job of Parish Clerk and teacher at the local charity school. This meant the family moved to the larger school house in Paulerspury. William would have had to attend church every week and here received a grounding in the Bible. He got a free education, which taught him how to read and write and introduced him to the wonderful world of books.

But the lanes and fields, and surrounding forest were his teachers too as he closely observed the flora and fauna, and in his bedroom built up a collection of specimens, alive and dead. Without realising it, he laid the foundations for becoming a great scientist. When he was twelve years old, he came across a 60 page Latin vocabulary and memorised all the words so that he could understand the Latin names of flowers, and In doing so he laid foundations for becoming a fine linguist too.

– bellis perennis

Another of his delights was learning about faraway places and reading about the adventures of explorers. When his Uncle Peter returned from Canada, he eagerly drank in all his traveller's tales. His fellow pupils nicknamed him Columbus, no doubt because of his passion for exploration and explorers.

When William was 14, his father obtained an apprenticeship for him as a cordwainer. This entailed learning how to make shoes in all their stages, as well as learning how to repair them. Clarke Nicholls of Piddington was chosen as his master and so began a period of more independence and a letting go of some of the Christian values of his childhood. But William Warr, a fellow-apprentice from Yardley Gobion, was determined to challenge him on matters of faith and church. He was the third generation in a family of dissenters and was gradually making faith his own. They would argue long and hard, with the result that Warr felt Carey was getting the better of him but Carey was increasingly more troubled by his conscience. Warr would bring books from home for him to read, and eventually persuaded him to go with him to the Meeting House at nearby Hackleton. It was here that Carey finally gave in, confessed his faith in Christ and joined the dissenters. He soon became a leader and helped to form this group of dissenting Christians into a church.

This conversion experience enlarged his mind in a new direction. He was keen to explore his new-found faith by listening to great preachers, and in reading the Bible and Christian books. Coming across Greek in New Testament commentaries he started teaching himself a new language. It was a time of exploring differences in Christian belief and practice and finding his own place. He met John Newton, vicar at Olney who, together with William Cowper, opened his eyes to the iniquity of the slave trade. Thomas Scott, also a vicar in the Olney area, as well as discussing matters of faith, would help him from time to time, with any difficulties he was experiencing with his Latin and Greek language study. John Sutcliff, the Baptist minister at Olney became a friend and mentor. A very memorable day was a visit to the Baptist Association Assembly at Olney. He had no money in his pocket. Someone gave him a glass of wine, but he feasted on three sermons, one of which was from Andrew Fuller of Kettering whom he had not previously met. Carey was entranced. Sutcliff ran a theological academy and in 1784 issued a 'Call to Prayer, to seek the revival of real religion and the extension of Christ's kingdom in the world'. This was obviously a big influence on William's thinking. At Hackleton he not only became a young church leader, but also a lay preacher, preaching there and in other village meeting houses. Before long he became convinced about believer's baptism and early one Sunday morning – 6th October 1783 - he walked into Northampton to be baptised in the River Nene. So began Carey's life as a Baptist and his absolute commitment to do God's will.

Life presented many challenges during his time in Piddington and Hackleton. Clarke Nichols of Piddington died before Carey had finished his apprenticeship and he transferred to Thomas Old in Hackleton. William fell in love with Dorothy Plackett, Old's sister-in-law, who also attended the Hackleton Meeting House. They were married in Piddington Church and later rejoiced in the birth of a baby girl, but she sadly died before reaching her second birthday. Thomas Old also died and left Carey to shoulder the burdens of the business and also the responsibility for his family. Poverty was ever knocking at their door and Carey tried his hand at teaching in the evenings.

> ' Before I formed you in the womb, I knew you,
> And before you were born I consecrated you;
> I appointed you a prophet to the nations.' Jeremiah 1:5

Q. How do we communicate to children the sense of excitement and adventure in being a follower of Jesus?

Q. Can you think of examples of how God works 'along the grain' of personality - interests, abilities, enthusiasms— when calling people to serve his kingdom's purposes?

Hackleton Meeting House

2. The big vision

'Without vision the people perish.' Proverbs 28:19

It seems likely that leaving Hackleton for Moulton felt like a fresh start for the couple and a huge adventure for Dorothy. William knew people at the Baptist Meeting House there who had probably told him there was a cobbler's cottage nearby which was available to rent and that the village schoolmaster had left the village. William was sure he could earn a living by opening a cottage school. He took with him all his beloved books and all his shoemaking tools, securing regular work making boots for Thomas Gotch in Kettering.

The Meeting House was just a stone's-throw from their cobbler's cottage, but the building had fallen into disrepair and having been without a minister for some time, the church was in decline. The members were elderly and discouraged. They did not meet every week. Imagine their delight at the arrival of this keen young couple! They knew William as a Baptist lay-preacher and asked him to preach for them. He promised them his free Sundays. It wasn't long before they were telling him they wished he would become their Minister. He was astonished at this idea, having had so little formal education. Another village chapel was also asking him to be their Minister. He decided to consult John Sutcliff, who suggested he should join them at Olney and put his call to the test with a trial sermon. This did not go well and the congregation turned him down, but added that he could try again the following year if he wished. In the meantime he became increasingly involved with the Moulton Meeting House and increasingly important to its people. The next year he did indeed have another attempt at preaching at Olney and this time they did agree to commission him as a Baptist minister. So he was ordained and inducted at Moulton in August 1787. He had broached with them the possibility of rebuilding the Meeting House and soon an appeal fund was launched. The appeal letter, endorsed by such people as John Ryland, Robert Hall, John Sutcliff, and Andrew Fuller, talked of the 'ruinous state of the building' and the danger of 'being buried alive'. Carey went far and wide with this letter, and eventually raised enough money—£100— to rebuild and extend the building. Extension was necessary because numbers were growing as young people in the village were finding faith under his ministry. There is no doubt that today Moulton owes its Baptist church to Carey's work during his four years there.

So Carey was very busy during his time at Moulton. He taught Dorothy to read and write as well as teaching his young paying pupils. In addition, he made and mended shoes and once a fortnight walked to Kettering with boots he'd made for Thomas Gotch, returning with rolls of leather for the next batch. If he were to become a minister, he must improve his education, so he worked on his Latin and New Testament Greek and added Hebrew. Reluctant to stop at dead languages, he taught himself French, Italian and Dutch. He created a wonderful garden, which was both hobby and necessity, because there was often no meat on the table and fruit and vegetables from the garden must have been very useful. Later on in India he would again turn to horticulture and agriculture to create greater diversity and food security. Ultimately he would be a chief founder and Secretary of 'The Agri-Horticultural Society of India'.

For teaching purposes he made both a wall map and a leather globe in order to inspire the school children with his wonder at the world. It seems that these objects affected him deeply. The world filled his mind and his thinking. Did not God love the whole world that he had made and all the people living in it? According to Matthew's Gospel, the last words Jesus said to his disciples were, 'Go into all the world and preach the Gospel.' He had started writing on his map what the Church had done since then and was appalled at how many times he had to write 'pagans' on his map. Jesus had promised to be with them to the end of the age, so surely that command applied to the Church of his day just as much as the promise did. It was an idea that just wouldn't go away. It was like a fire burning within him and it seemed he talked about it wherever he went. The hyper-Calvinism prevailing at the time found such ideas presumptuous; it was for God to call his elect, in his own good time. Carey got Moulton to join in with Sutcliff's initiative of the monthly Call to Prayer. Some dismissed him as 'an enthusiast'. There were others sympathetic to the idea of world mission, but to whom it seemed an unrealistic dream. Praying for it was one thing: setting about such an enterprise was another matter altogether. Dissenters tended to be poor and less well educated than those in the Church of England. Carey would dearly have liked world mission to be an ecumenical venture, but he felt the time was not right. However, within a decade other denominations would be following where Baptists had led.

In 1934 Carey's great grandson, S. Pearce Carey visited Moulton and when stepping inside the cottage, declared, 'This was Carey's Troas!' It was as if his globe and map talked to him every bit as much as Paul's vision at Troas (Acts 16:8-10) had led to the Gospel first being proclaimed in what is now Europe.

When appealing for money to rebuild the meeting house, he was visiting Birmingham. One fellow Baptist and a businessman there – Thomas Potts - told him he should write down his ideas and then people would take them seriously. Carey's reply was that he'd had such a poor education, he didn't think he could write a book. 'If you cannot do it as you wish, do it as you are able,' came back the reply. Having tried and failed to get his older friends to take on the task, Carey took this advice and started writing his 'Enquiry' while still at Moulton. It was to be a slim book with a fashionably long title: 'An Enquiry into the obligations of Christians to use means for the conversion of the heathens, in which the religious state of the nations of the world, the success of former undertakings , and the practicability of further undertakings are considered.' Much of the statistical information came from his wall map. Extensive research led him to discover what people like Jonathan Edwards and Brainerd had done recently in America, and Moravian missionaries too, who had had such an influence on the Wesley brothers. In the book he shared his ideas of how such a huge task could be tackled. The writing continued when he and his family moved to Leicester.

Three boys were born to them at Moulton – Felix, William and Peter. Family finances were meagre. As the Minister at Moulton he was paid less than a farm labourer earned. It was not surprising therefore that when he was offered the opportunity to be the Minister at Harvey Lane, Leicester, having agonised over the decision for over a month, he felt he should accept. Moving to a new church brought serious pastoral challenges. Moving to a large town brought new stimulus and opportunities. He met scientists and philosophers, people who would invite him into their libraries and allow him to borrow their books. He got involved with prison reform and improving the care of the mentally ill. He became an activist to improve opportunities for dissenters and met others fighting against the slave trade. As a family they were supporting the sugar boycott because sugar was the product of slave labour.

Yes, Leicester was certainly a time of growth and development. We see evidence of this In May 1792 when Carey was invited to address church leaders and representatives at the Association meetings at Friar Lane Nottingham. His 'Enquiry' had been printed and was on sale. In his sermon he poured out all his dreams and aspirations for world mission. The sermon had two points: 'Expect great things from God: Attempt great things for God.' His text was Isaiah 54:2 about extending your tent and strengthening the stakes. Afterwards people were congratulating him on a good sermon, but as they began to change the subject, he turned to Andrew Fuller and, tugging his sleeve he said, 'Sir, is still nothing going to be *done?*' Fuller paused before suggesting, 'We meet in Kettering in October and we will see if we can form a society.' Carey's world view was indeed expanding rapidly. Could his vision now be on the way to becoming a reality?

'Go therefore and make disciples of all nations, baptising them in the name of the Father, and of the Son and of the Holy Spirit, and teaching them to obey everything that I have commanded you. And remember: I am with you to the end of the age.' Matthew 28:19,20

Q. The Bible begins with one couple in relationship with God and ends with people of every tribe and nation: does the Church still suffer from low expectations and limited vision?

Q. How do we encourage our Christian community to see the bigger picture and think globally? Does it matter?

The 'Enquiry'

3. Obedience

'Commit your way to the Lord; trust in him and he will act.' Psalm 37:6

There were times when Carey seems to have been very sure of what God's will for him was. He knew he had to accept Jesus as his Saviour and Lord as a seventeen year old. He knew he must become a dissenter, however painful that was. He'd grown up despising dissenters and he did feel a sense of shame in joining them, but then, he thought, that was nothing compared with the shame Jesus experienced in being crucified. Although baptised as an infant, he became convinced baptism as a believer was a question of obedience and when he walked into Northampton early that Sunday morning in October 1783, it was a crucial moment in his Christian life: he was committing himself to obey God's will, whatever that might entail. John Collett Ryland had got his son John Ryland Jnr. to meet him in the vestry of Philip Doddridge's church on Castle Hill. At 6 o'clock that morning, they made their way down to the River Nene, with just a handful of people to witness his baptism there. The river has been re-routed to make way for the Railway Station, and there are few signs of the castle walls left, but the station does have a plaque commemorating this event. The cobbler from Hackleton and the baptising Minister had no idea that they were destined to work very closely together in the future work of world mission, and until the end of John Ryland's life.

Some challenges took Carey by surprise, such as the call to be a Baptist minister. Both Moulton and Earls Barton were asking him to become their minister. Was this really from God? Lay-preaching was one thing, but surely you needed a good education to be a minister, and he was all too aware how basic his own had been. His instinct was to consult John Sutcliff, Minister of the Baptist Church at Olney. He was an older Christian whom Carey had admired and trusted since his conversion. Following his advice he had preached a trial sermon to the large and daunting congregation at Olney and been turned down. You might have expected him to deduce this was God's guiding and the closing of a door. But Olney had left the door open for him to reapply the following year, if he wished. Moulton welcomed and appreciated his service and he had become their unofficial minister, so try again he did. Although he was not at all happy with his sermon on this occasion either, Olney did in fact commission him 'to preach wherever God in his providence should call him to go.' So the support of Moulton and the commissioning of Olney were the factors that confirmed for him that this was indeed God's calling to which he must say 'yes', however inadequate he felt. He was ordained and formally inducted at Moulton in August 1787. This led to his redoubled attempts to improve his education by wide reading and study of the languages of the Bible.

Later, in October 1792, as promised by Andrew Fuller in May, a meeting took place in Kettering, in Widow Wallis's back parlour. Twelve men sat round a table and said, "We'll do it! We'll form a society: 'The Particular Baptist Society for the Propagation of the Gospel among the Heathen'." They would need to raise funds. Further meetings were arranged. Carey had set his heart on Tahiti and the South Sea islands having read Captain Cook's journals of his voyages which had revealed so much need in that area of the world. Captain Cook had mused on how unlikely it was that missionaries would go there because there would be little advantage for them. Carey was stung by this: how could Cook think that missionaries would only go somewhere for monetary gain! People said they never heard Carey pray without praying for these islanders.

But then John Thomas came on the scene. He wrote to Carey saying he had spent some time in India, initially as a ship's doctor, but then for a while working in Bengal as a missionary. He was wanting to return but was looking to find a colleague to go with him. He'd heard about what had happened in Kettering – in fact he'd meant to come along but had forgotten what time the meeting was. Please would Carey ask the newly-formed mission committee if they could help him. He spoke Bengali fluently. The Committee was interested but cautious and made enquiries. Thomas was invited to their third meeting but failed to turn up until business was over. He'd damaged his foot. They re-opened the meeting to interview him. He was questioned about the cost of living in India and about how easy it was to gain employment. He assured them everything was very cheap and employment readily available. They failed to recognise the romanticised nature of this view, and this led Carey to volunteer to be that colleague. Thomas immediately rushed to give him an excited hug and this was to clinch the matter. If only they had been able to talk to people who'd been with Thomas in India they would have learned just how impractical and unpredictable was this warm Christian man with such a heart for India. They would have learned about his inability to handle money and how easily he fell into debt; they would have learned about his wild projects that came to nothing and his ability to offend people. S. Pearce Carey sums him up: 'He dragged a maimed self, ever game but lame, warrior but weakling. However there were none to warn, so that meeting ended with a feeling of great excitement for all.'

But this was the point where reality began to hit home as Carey returned to tell his wife to what he'd committed himself. She was two months from giving birth and it became clear he would have to leave without her. She was very distressed and begged him not to go, fearful of what might happen to him. The following Sunday he told his church. To say that Harvey Lane members were very sad to lose him as their minister is to understate it. They had known such blessing and growth in the last year and there were many tears. Leaving his father and siblings, as well as his many friends, was another source of sadness. He wrote to his father, "I hope, dear Father you will be enabled to surrender me up to the Lord. I have many sacrifices to make. I must part with a beloved family, and a number of most affectionate friends. Never did I see such sorrow manifested as reigned through our place of worship last Sunday. But I have set my hand to the plough." It was a very difficult time emotionally. Gifts poured into the Mission, thanks to the enthusiasm of the Committee and some others, but many ministerial colleagues were very sceptical of the venture and doubted its timing and prospect of success.

William was utterly convinced that this was what God wanted him to do, and after a while Dorothy accepted it, so they made a plan: Dorothy would move back to Piddington to live with sister Kitty and to be near to her other relatives. Sons William and Peter would stay with her and she would have her baby there. Their eldest son Felix would go with his father to India and in three years' time they would return, having made a home in India. Hopefully Dorothy would then be willing to return with them, together with their two other sons and the new sibling who would be a three year old child.

But it was not easy for Carey and Felix with Thomas and his family to get a passage to India. The East India Company did not want missionaries in India and did their best to obstruct them. Also, Thomas was in debt and creditors were trying to prevent him from leaving the country until debts were paid. One ship left without them. This meant that the baby was born while they were still in the country and William wrote to Dorothy from the Isle of Wight expressing his delight to hear of her safe delivery. He asked her to tell him what she had called their 'dear little child'. Among all the chat about people they'd met, meals eaten, and enjoyment of Felix' company, William confessed to her, 'If I had all the world I would gladly give it all to be with you and my dear family, but I could not turn back without guilt on my soul.' The letter proves how costly it was to leave Dorothy and all those he loved for three years, but it also confirms his conviction that he was going to India in the belief it was in obedience to God's call and he could not put anything or anyone before the God to whom he'd pledged absolute allegiance at his baptism. Then the story takes a different turn: Carey persuades Thomas to accompany him back to Piddington, while they are waiting for a Danish ship to take them on their voyage. He is daring to hope that now the baby has been born -Jabez -Dorothy might be willing to join them. Unsurprisingly the answer is still 'no', so there is a second painful goodbye. When Thomas sees how upset William is, he decides to go back inside and see if he can persuade Dorothy to change her mind. Under his pressure, she says she'll go if her sister Kitty comes too. After a quick pray, Kitty agrees to go. Within two days they have packed up and are on their way to the coast on their big adventure. Kitty is the only one who will ever return to England.

Life in India would present Carey with many difficult decisions to be made. One important decision came after being there for seven years when he was invited by the East India Company to work at their Fort William College in

Calcutta. It was a secular job and a new initiative, inducting their young employees into the culture and languages of India to fit them for high office in the civil service. They had sought in vain for a more respectable candidate to take the job as Professor of Bengali, in other words, an Anglican with a good education. It would be some time before they could bring themselves to call a dissenter 'Professor', but Carey was clearly the best man for the job. It was a good wage, and the offer came when members of the new missionary community at Serampore were each considering how they could contribute financially to the work of the mission. Carey agonised over whether to accept the position, feeling utterly daunted and inadequate. Was this of God? It is unsurprising that he doubted his ability to do the job. But he was also concerned about whether or not this was part of God's plan for him. He found his answer in consulting his missionary colleagues, who encouraged him to accept. There is no doubt this resulted in him exerting a great influence on a whole generation of young men entering important jobs in the English administration, perhaps curbing some excesses. He would meet with them for extra-mural discussions of a Christian nature. Many became Christians and later would appeal to the Serampore Mission to send mission workers to where they found themselves working. There is a nice irony in this largely self-educated weaver's son becoming Professor of Bengali, Sanskrit, and Marathi and teaching members of the English aristocracy, public schoolboys, likely to have been educated at Oxford and Cambridge universities, when he himself had never stepped inside a university or experienced anything but a village charity school!

One of his gifts to Bengali culture during a long period in this post was that he took traditional tales from their oral tradition and gave them a literary form as teaching materials. Holding this post also meant that he was able to obtain the services of some of the ablest Indian scholars to help him with translating the bible and in compiling dictionaries and grammars in different languages. In addition they would translate works into Bengali and create their own literary works which were foundational for Bengali literature. When Carey first went to India, Bengali was just a vernacular language. He is credited as a prime mover in it becoming the literary language it is today.

The salary was enormously useful in funding church, school and university building projects, as well as funding the printing and publishing business and employing Indian workmen for a whole variety of work for the mission. It also funded Indian Christians in mission outposts far and wide.

We see how one way that Carey sought to know God's will was through consulting fellow Christians. There were also times his convictions led him to independent decisions. One such decision, following Dorothy's death in 1807, was to marry the Danish aristocrat Charlotte Rumohr with what seemed to the Serampore community - undue haste. They wrote him a round-robin imploring him not to marry Charlotte. She was a frail invalid and they could only believe she would be a hindrance to him and to the Mission. Caring for Dorothy had been hard for them all and no doubt this plan gave them a sense of *déjà vu*. But marry her he did and so began a blissful relationship which brought great joy to both parties and an injection of considerable wealth into the work of the Mission! Charlotte may have been physically frail, but her supportiveness for her husband and for their work was a great asset. Sadly she died in 1821. Carey was married yet again, to Grace Hughes who lovingly cared for him to the end of his life.

'The Lord is King! I own his power,
his right to rule each day and hour;
I own his claim on heart and will,
and his demands I would fulfil.'
- Darley Terry

Q. Does the call of God always include sacrifice? Is it fair if an individual's sacrifice entails sacrifice for others too?

Q. Abraham believed God was commanding him to sacrifice his son; Carey believed God wanted him to leave wife and family, or ask them to leave the security of home for India. They were men of their respective ages. How can we be sure about the will of God and his purpose for our lives in this age?

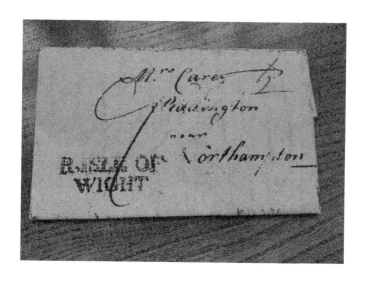

William's letter to Dorothy following the birth of Jabez

4. Time management

'Conduct yourselves wisely...making the most of the time.' Colossians 4:5

Carey must have been gifted with great energy when we consider all he fitted into life. At Moulton he'd been husband and father, school teacher, shoe-maker and cobbler, preacher and pastor, church-rebuilder, garden-maker, student of six languages, author, teacher of Dorothy. When Andrew Fuller had visited him to welcome him into the fraternity of Baptist ministers he had been astounded at how busy Carey was.

'And don't you make boots for my deacon, Thomas Gotch?' he had asked. When Fuller next saw Gotch, he chided him for making money out of this hard-working young minister. When Carey next went to Kettering with the latest batch of boots he'd made, he was called into the parlour where Gotch asked him how much he earned a week from this work.

'It's about nine or ten shillings a week, Sir,' replied Carey.

'Very well,' said Gotch, and with a twinkle, 'From now on I shall give you ten shillings from my private purse, and I will not have you spoiling any more of my leather! Then you will be able to get on with your studies.'

I suspect Carey would have used his long, fortnightly walks to Kettering and back for reading or mastering vocabulary or grammar for his language study, but no doubt Gotch's generosity saved him many hours for his other pursuits. The economic demands of his growing family meant he continued teaching even when the village schoolmaster returned and he lost some of his pupils. We know his shoe-making and mending continued too.

At Leicester he was also very busy. As well as his shoemaking he also kept a school. The ministerial stipend was larger than at Moulton but he was on probation for two years. The church had lots of demanding problems which taxed the wisdom of such a young minister and made him very distressed at times. However his tactics did eventually lead to harmony and growth. He had a pattern of study: Mondays the classics; Tuesdays science and history; the other days it was Hebrew Bible and Greek New Testament studies for his mid-week and Sunday sermons. Most days he would study a Hebrew psalm. He also preached in Leicestershire villages. He was Secretary of the

Nonconformist Committee, fighting against discriminatory laws. Friends drew him into action for prison reform and exploring new ideas for the care of the mentally ill. He met great scientists of his day and engaged in discussion with the intelligentsia of Leicester. His concern for the slave trade increased as he found out more from people like William Wilberforce and the Clapham Sect. He delighted in access to the libraries of friends and they discussed books like Thomas Paine's 'Rights of Man'. How did he fit it all in to a mere 24 hours a day?

It is fairly certain he revelled in the five-month long voyage to India on the Kron Princessa Maria, and he put that time to good use in getting Thomas to teach him Bengali, and in helping Thomas begin to translate Genesis into Bengali. Carey invited passengers to join them in their cabin for morning and evening worship and for Sunday services.

All his life in India, he adopted a pattern for each day to work at his different projects. In his Journals he bemoans his laziness. It is very hard to find evidence for this! He was a prolific letter-writer and many of his letters survive. In addition to his journals, he wrote Periodic Accounts for the Society at home. But his work of translation of the Bible into Indian languages and dialects is perhaps his most staggering achievement. It started with the Bengali New Testament, and then Hindi. It was important to learn Sanskrit which was the basis of other Indian languages. But then, what about Marathi and Oriya, Persian, Telegu? The whole Bible was translated into six Indian languages and parts of the Bible – the Psalms or the Gospels – into 29 other languages. He was never content and they were constantly being revised. The Bengali Bible went into several revised editions. He completed the eighth revision of the New Testament not long before his death and it was part of a new single volume Bengali Bible. He compiled dictionaries and grammars; wrote text books for the schools they opened – fee-paying boarding schools for Europeans and free schools for Bengali children. Of course, he did not do this alone. Both missionary colleagues and native speakers and scholars of the different languages, or 'pundits', were all involved in the projects. One of his great strengths was that he was very much a 'team player'. It is a tribute to him that people were only too happy to contribute to this great work. He always regarded them as works in progress, wanting others after him to improve them. Later, when they founded Serampore University, he would write text books on many subjects for its students: forestry, agriculture, botany, geology, astronomy. He edited and published Roxburgh's massive works 'Hortus Bengalensis' and his three volume 'Flora Indica'. Then there were the newspapers the Mission Press produced: the English language 'Friend of India' and the Bengali ones which were the first in an Indian language. There was always a new project being developed such as lending libraries, or savings schemes to offer loans at reasonable rates of interest. The vision of the Serampore Mission just kept growing.

Although Carey was only in Calcutta for a few days each week, he wasn't content to be just a professor at Fort William College. He opened a preaching place in one of the poorest areas of the city, Lall Bazar, where sailors from many countries met to relax on land. Eventually this became a union church run by both BMS and LMS. Carey felt limited by time constraints but each Thursday evening he would have an open house to enquirers, and those coming were many. He always felt others much better at evangelism than him, but dealing with seekers after truth was his delight. Later on, a boat was commissioned for a mission to seamen there.

Carey's abiding hobby all through life was gardening, from helping his Uncle Peter in Paulerspury to being wheeled round his five acre garden in Serampore towards the end of his life. When living in the school house as a child he had had his own plot, and in every home he had, however temporary, he would always be found creating a garden. Food grown was often a necessity when times were hard. This passion was perhaps the one thing that gave him a work-leisure balance and was good exercise too. It also provided him with a specially created sanctuary in which he would daily commune with his Maker. His Serampore garden was laid out like a botanical garden with plants arranged according to their Linnaean classification. He was always begging people to send him seeds, bulbs, corms, saplings and would give instructions for packaging so that they would withstand the journey. His letters reveal the impressive depth and extent of his botanical knowledge. People sent these precious packages from all manner of different locations in different countries. He had a magnificent collection and also shared treasures with others, especially with notable horticulturalists of the period and botanical gardens in Calcutta, Liverpool, Edinburgh, and Kew Gardens. He would employ Indian artists to make botanical drawings too. One day, he had emptied a sack of neatly packaged and carefully labelled seeds from England and found some loose seeds at the bottom. He carefully shook the seeds over a spare piece of ground. Returning some days later he found - to his inexpressible delight - some specimens of *bellis perennis* growing there: English daisies!

'Lord I have time, I have plenty of time, all the time that you give me, the years of my life, the days of my years, the hours of my days, mine to fill, quietly, calmly , but to fill completely, up to the brim, to offer to you, that of their insipid water you may make a rich wine such as you made once at Cana of Galilee....'

Michel Quoist

Q. If our time is a finite gift of God, how can we be better stewards of it? Some people keep an account of the proportions of time spent on different activities, in order to decide whether or not they are content with priorities and life-balance.

Q. Why do we complain about 'no time', 'too little time', 'time rushing by'?

The sister ship of the Kron Princessa Maria

20

5. When the going gets tough

'In this world you will have trouble, but take heart:
I have overcome the world.' John 16:33

As a young boy growing up in Paulerspury, William had once fallen from an oak tree and hurt himself quite badly. His mother gave him a good telling-off for being so foolish; he with his short little legs! But when he had recovered, the first thing he did was to conquer that tree. This determination not to give in or accept defeat would characterise his behaviour throughout his life. Perseverance was a quality he had in abundance. His sister Mary said of him, 'Whatever he began, he finished. Difficulties never discouraged him.'

Perhaps the first really difficult time the young William experienced was when he was apprenticed to the cordwainer, Clarke Nichols, who was very demanding and hot-tempered, especially when drunk. Life was not easy, but worse was to come; he died before William had finished his apprenticeship. Thomas Old gladly took him on as a journeyman shoemaker, initially at reduced pay. Carey married his employer's sister-in-law, Dorothy, and their happiness turned to anguish when their first daughter died from fever. William too suffered from fever for a prolonged period which resulted in premature baldness. After four years, Thomas Old died too and Carey was left with the responsibilities of caring for his widowed sister-in-law and her four children, and also for running the business. One customer in particular took advantage of the new young manager and left him in dire financial straits. William redoubled his efforts to sell shoes and to buy and sell refurbished ones. He also opened an evening school but struggled to escape poverty. So his time at Piddington and Hackleton presented many difficult challenges. Money was always in short supply at Moulton too and even initially at Leicester.

Harvey Lane, Leicester had proved a very difficult church to start with. There had been three ministers in the course of the previous three years and the last one was not only forced to resign but had his membership withdrawn. Initially things went well but then dissension and strife returned with a vengeance. Eventually Carey dissolved the membership and invited a new membership to sign a covenant. Those who refused, angrily threatened trouble, but gradually Carey won them over. Healing and growth came, such that the church was utterly distraught to receive his news that he was leaving for India.

John Thomas had estimated what it would cost to live in India for a year, by which time they intended to be self-financing. This turned out to be a gross underestimate. He was in charge of the money and had spent it all within just over a month, with a degree of profligacy and little wisdom. They found themselves homeless and hungry. Initially the Carey family were offered a dilapidated garden house but then were fortunate to be offered land – rent-free for three years – in a village in the Sunderbans with a bungalow nearby which they could occupy. It was a three day journey by river to get there, with both Dorothy and Felix ill with fever. When they arrived at the bungalow, they found it was not in fact unoccupied, but lived in by salt-merchant Charles Short. Their hearts must have sunk, but then he urged them to stay and offered them wonderful hospitality. William had a real sense of God's provision and began to enjoy the more rural environment despite the fact that it was an area where tigers cost many human lives each year, and there were many poisonous snakes and hungry crocodiles. He was by now able to share his faith with people in the neighbourhood. He was cultivating the land and building the family their own house. But just as Carey had almost finished this building, he heard from John Thomas that he had started working for a Christian owner of an indigo plantation and had secured a similar management job for him too, in Mudnabati less than twenty miles away from where he himself was. This too belonged to Mr Udny who was most sympathetic to their Christian mission. This seemed too good an offer to turn down, but it did mean a 300 mile river trip which took twenty three days. It also meant leaving Kitty behind, because she had fallen in love with the salt merchant and they were engaged to be married. That must have been especially hard for Dorothy.

The new job brought in a good income with a very pleasant house to go with it. With his botanical interest, Carey found training for the process of producing dye from the indigo plants fascinating. Work was seasonal and left plenty of time for mastering Bengali, learning Hindustani and Sanskrit, translating the Bible and working as an evangelist in the area. Then disaster struck. Malaria was rife and five year old Peter succumbed to the fever and sadly died. To add to their grief, it was extremely difficult to get either Hindus or Muslims to provide any assistance with his burial. Poor Dorothy. Her mental health deteriorated. She was indeed paying a heavy price for agreeing to accompany her husband to this country. Both she and William became increasingly lonely. It was advised that having another baby would help Dorothy and she gave birth to Jonathan. It did not help.

Furthermore, William received a letter from the home Society's Treasurer expressing disapproval at the apparent pursuit of wealth to the detriment of their mission. This stung him deeply. He was sensitive to the fact that although the indigenous people congregated in great numbers to listen to him preaching – sometimes as many as 500 – none had been willing to commit to becoming a Christian. They listened with great interest and responded warmly, but custom and astrology were everything. However, Europeans were finding faith and commitment and a small church was established. Carey had no doubt there would be an Indian church one day but he began to think his job was just to prepare the way.

He had appealed to the Society to send more missionaries to join him and great was his delight when in October 1796 John Fountain arrived in Mudnabati. They found they had so much in common and worked very well together. They heard of a printing press for sale in Calcutta but it was very expensive. When George Udny heard about it, to their immense delight, he bought it for them. Following a very bad season with severe flooding which ruined the indigo, Udni decided to abandon the indigo works. He was rather exasperated too by John Thomas giving up on his other indigo plantation and having moved away. Carey decided that he would himself invest in another plantation on higher ground some distance away. This would provide a good source of income for the mission. News came that other missionaries were on the way and they began preparations to build accommodation for them.

One day however, William Ward came to visit them with the report that the new recruits had arrived but were being refused entry on to British ruled territory. Serampore, however, which was under Danish rule, was prepared to welcome them and allow them to establish their mission work there. This was another very hard decision to be made, but clearly, moving to Serampore had to be the right thing to do, and so it turned out. A school, the church and other ventures were left in the hands of the European Christian friends, but Carey left a big hole in the community and made a considerable loss on his investment. It was very hard leaving that area. Hard too to leave Peter's grave. Yet again, everything was packed up, and into the boat, including the precious printing press and very many plants. It was the first day of the new century - 1800. Ten days later they all arrived in Serampore. The Danish Governor, Colonel Bie, was very sympathetic to the idea of Christian mission, and would prove to be a valuable supporter.

The next decade was very fruitful in many ways, but 1812 saw a new catastrophe: the great fire that destroyed their printing works. More about that later. We shall return to other tough times too. Misunderstandings and mischief-spreading by a new generation of missionaries, schism from the home society, more deaths, banking crashes and losing all their money, floods that damaged property.- all these were indeed tough times that lay ahead.

> When you pass through the waters, I will be with you;
> and through the rivers, they shall not overwhelm you;
> when you walk through fire, you shall not be burned,
> and the flame shall not consume you. Isaiah 43:2

Q. Indigo production is seen today as having been an exploitative colonial practice. What will be seen in future centuries to have been the blind spots of our country in this age?

Q, When bad things happened, Carey's age understood them as God's way of teaching them lessons such as humility and dependency. If today we would think of God being the source of all that is good, how do we explain these bad things?

Q. Do we value the qualities of persistence in difficult circumstance and 'stickability' in our time?

In Memoriam Peter Carey

6. Community living

'Now the whole group of those who believed were of one heart and soul, and no one claimed private ownership of any possessions, but everything they owned was held in common.' - Acts 4:32

The first seven years in India were in many ways difficult and lonely. John Thomas was unpredictable: a free spirit who would come and go. Dorothy's deteriorating mental health created different challenges as she turned on those closest to her. But the new century's dawning saw the start of a new chapter with the move to Serampore. Having missionary colleagues brought great delight to Carey who had long cherished the idea of a Christian community similar to those enjoyed by Moravians. With the arrival of several missionary families this now became a possibility. Not that this would be easy. Ward had told of clashes and conflict on their voyage to India. When they arrived in Serampore and met everyone, it was obvious this was still a problem, even to the point of people coming to physical blows! But Carey would prove the catalyst for unity and concord. They would stay together until death parted them. Sadly Grant had already died on arrival. Both Fountain and Brunsdon would last only a few months after coming to Serampore before they too died. This left just three families – Ward, the Careys and the Marshmans – who would stay together for many years, growing closer and ever more united in purpose.

They naturally looked to Carey as the expert and leaned on him, ready to accept him as their leader. But he was determined that their community should be utterly democratic; a family of equals. Carey was utterly courteous and deferential. He secretly vowed that he would never be the conscious occasion of friction. No one should be called Master because only Christ was their Master. All the important tasks would be done by each one by monthly rotation. Every Saturday evening they met to discuss concerns and to settle any difference that might have occurred during the week. Any hurt must be mentioned then. Not to do so would be considered very serious They all took turns in leading the weekly English service. This was all very different from the Moravian pattern.

The basic principle of the community was that there should be no trading or working for personal gain. Their life-style would be frugal and all earnings would be pooled and apportioned according to need, with all the surplus being invested in the work of the Mission. They would each use their particular talents to fund this way of life and purpose. The publication of the Bible in Bengali was the immediate priority, so Carey and Fountain would provide the clear copy for Ward who with the help of Felix and Brunsdon would typeset it for printing ready for proof reading. To fund this expensive process the mission press would take commissions to earn money. Hannah and Joshua Marshman would open fee-paying boarding schools for European children. Hannah also became the community's effective mother who would hold everything together through good times and bad. She would deal with workmen, and tradespeople and the efficient day-to-day running of the community. There was also much building work to be undertaken and overseen. Hannah would outlive them all. She would be assisted by Mrs Fountain on the catering side, who a year after her husband's death married William Ward.

Within four months, their building work was complete and they met to hold a day of thanksgiving when Carey was confirmed as Pastor. Colonel Bie joined in enthusiastically. At about this time John Thomas turned up to join them.

Carey was so happy to live in community and Dorothy benefitted greatly from having others to care for her. She had become paranoid about her husband and he found it difficult to help her because she constantly railed at him and even attacked him for his imagined unfaithfulness. It got to the stage where she had to be confined to her room, so unruly was her behaviour in the streets. Everyone enjoyed having the school children boarding with them. Felix in particular really benefitted from Ward's fatherly care. Marshman commented that he had turned him from a tiger into a lamb. He and his brothers missed out on mothering and it would seem their father was very poor at discipline. Being too preoccupied with matters outside of the family was perhaps one of Carey's chief failings. Gradually they were all becoming welded into a loving community which shared a common purpose.

But the community was far from exclusive. Hannah would welcome many local women who wanted her help, both practical and advisory. John Thomas' medical skills were much in demand and in fact their very first Indian convert came to faith as a result of John Thomas resetting his dislocated shoulder. All of them were able to learn from him in improving their own first aid skills and people knew they would find such help from the community. Many people worked for them, from builders to translators, from gardeners to punch makers creating movable type for the printing press. The core people in the community were Carey, Ward, and Marshman. They would be referred to as the Serampore Trio. (Hannah was 'just' a missionary's wife!) Their good relationship and the way they complemented one another was truly remarkable. The secret lay in the fact that each esteemed the other more highly than themself.

Community living certainly gave a degree of freedom to them as individuals, especially Carey who for 29 years would spend part of each week in Calcutta. Foreign trips were made possible because of shared responsibilities. There were also economies of scale and there is no doubt far more was achieved by their working together than could have been achieved otherwise. They all worked hard and were accountable to one another. It was possible to cope with a stream of people visiting them and wanting to stay. Some were people with an interest in Bible translation like Johannes Lassar who was a master of Mandarin. He stayed for some time to teach the language to Marshman and others in order for them to add Chinese to their Bible translation work. Anglican chaplain Henry Martyn had been inspired by stories of Carey to become a missionary/chaplain himself and a close friendship and collaboration ensued. After visiting Carey in Calcutta, he was invited to Serampore and lived nearby for some time. The first time he visited Serampore he was surprised to be sitting down to eat with 150 others! Adoniram Judson and his wife Ann, were also entertained briefly by Carey in Calcutta and then for several months in Serampore as they awaited permission to go to Burma where they would work with Felix. Indeed many missionaries belonging to other societies and denominations came to visit and stay awhile to benefit from their experience and advice. Everyone enjoyed and admired Carey's five acre garden. There were many who beat a trail to Serampore to learn more about the Christian faith. Some were converts in search of fresh teaching, having become Christians from brief encounters with Carey and others over the years. How difficult such hospitality would have been without the community and especially people like Mary Ward who soon took on the role of being in charge of the catering, alongside Hannah Marshman who shouldered so many responsibilities.

But we return to March 1812 and the catastrophe of the fire. It had already been a sad year with five deaths among the Serampore community, including the Wards' daughter and a baby son born to the Marshmans. The fire took hold just after the workers had all gone home at the end of the day, which meant no one lost their life in the blaze. For four hours Marshman and Ward organised water carriers to douse the flames. Boarders had to be evacuated from their dormitories. The printing presses were saved but 1000 reams of newly delivered paper, the moveable type in all the different fonts and many precious manuscripts were destroyed, together with everything else in the building. At midnight the roof beams collapsed and the fire re-ignited which resulted in an anxious two hours, praying it would not spread to surrounding buildings. By 2 a.m. it seemed it had burnt itself out and they could snatch a little sleep before Marshman went to Calcutta at dawn to tell Carey what had happened.

The shock was immense, but there was never any thought of giving up. It was Carey's grammars, dictionaries and other manuscripts which were the chief loss that no amount of money could restore. He vowed they would be better next time. Arriving back at Serampore they found a jubilant Ward who, while clearing debris, had found the precious punches used for casting the type, buried but uninjured. These had taken skilled Indian craftsmen ten years to make. The melted metal could be salvaged. They called a meeting of all their employees, and set pundits to work repairing damaged manuscripts and type-casters to their work. Others were paid a month's wage and sent home to return in one month to start work again. Doing an inventory of losses they calculated it at between £9,000 and £10,000. When the news hit

Britain, the outpouring of sympathy and generosity was enormous. Even Moulton gave £50 which would have been Carey's pay there for five years! Many churches and many individuals joined in, and not just Baptists. In the end, Ryland, Sutcliff and Fuller had to declare the fund closed. Suddenly people began to realise the scale and extent of what was being accomplished in far-off India. Fuller trembled for their new-found celebrity. Carey and his colleagues were very chastened by the experience but found much for which to be grateful. By working hard as a team, the Mission Press was indeed fully operational again after two months.

'How very good and pleasant it is when kindred live together in unity!'
Psalm 133:1

Q. Many Christians today find living together in community with shared values and purposes enriches their lives and multiplies their effectiveness in mission. How aware are we of what is happening in our local area? What are the advantages and disadvantages of community living?

Q. We speak of churches being Christian communities: how could our own church become a richer and more effective community?

Q. Increasingly there are virtual Christian communities. Some are like traditional churches and some more like monastic communities. Is this development something to be embraced or regretted?

Hannah Marshman
1767-1847

Joshua Marshman

1768-1837

William Ward
1769-1823

7. Misunderstandings and opposition

'If it is possible, so far as it depends on you, live peaceably with all.'
Romans 12:18

It is people rather than circumstances that can bring the greatest challenges. No one faced more devastating opposition from friends and fellow countrymen than those early Indian Christian converts. Carey and others wept with them, supported them and did all they could to help. How they had rejoiced at their baptisms and to see their eagerness to learn more and to share their new-found faith! How touched they were to see their fortitude in the face of terrible persecution! But there was also a time of disappointment when there was rudeness, bullying, lying, indiscretion, and turning away. Carey had sleepless nights over it. There was bad behaviour from sons Felix and William too, when some time had passed since their commitment to faith and baptism. But eventually contrition and forgiveness restored good fellowship. Krishna Pal—the first Indian convert— went on to become a very faithful and effective evangelist.

From the earliest days, the East India Company and British authorities had made life difficult for the missionaries going to India, and on arrival there. Things had changed under the Governor General, Lord Wellesley, who appointed Carey to Fort William College. He had allowed preaching in Lall Bazar the poorest and most cosmopolitan area of Calcutta - and the work of the mission in that city had begun to spread. It was at Wellesley's request that Carey had researched infanticide statistics in order to make it illegal. But governor generals move on and new ones take their place. One acting governor general and then Lord Minto were particularly difficult. They put a stop to public preaching in Calcutta, forbade preaching to Indians, tried to put a stop to new missionaries arriving and tried to get the Mission Press to move to Calcutta where they could keep a close eye on it. The Serampore community was forbidden to send out Indian Christians to evangelise elsewhere. This was quite heart-breaking for them all. One new missionary was sent to Burma to reconnoitre possibilities of working there instead and they even considered moving the whole Mission there. Carey obtained an audience with the new Danish Governor who forbade the removal of the Mission Press. Then Carey and Marshman were granted an audience with Lord Minto. He warmed to them but suggested it was wrong to try and make Indians Christians. Carey replied, 'You mistake us, your lordship. We have no faith *in makings*. You can make hypocrites by compulsion: Christians never.' Restrictions were not immediately lifted but the stipulation about the Mission Press moving to Calcutta was dropped.

There was also opposition in the Parliament in London. Fuller and others worked to great effect to marshal support when a bill was introduced calling for the recall of the missionary community from Bengal. The East India Company's Charter review took place in 1813. In answer to five speeches against the Mission, Wilberforce was among a number of MPs who spoke powerfully in their support as did Lord Wellesley in the House of Lords. The bill was defeated and the Charter included a stipulation that support should be given to those going to India who were seeking 'to promote happiness, religious and moral improvement'. This was to mark the end of restrictions on the work of the Mission, and the way was now open for the sending of reinforcements. Even powerful people in the English administration, some of whom had been Carey's students at Fort William College, were wanting them to send missionaries to where they were working. It was a great encouragement to the Serampore Mission.

But circumstances were also changing for the worse – much worse. In 1814 Sutcliff died and Fuller the following year. They had been such vital friends and supporters. They had shared together with Carey, Marshman and Ward the big vision and everything that had happened. They had considered themselves 'rope-holders' to the pioneers going down a deep well, or pit, into the unknown in search of buried treasure. Their support had always been magnificent as well as their work of advocacy and explanation to people in the churches and the denomination at large. But now, instead of a committee of virtually three, it became enlarged to 35. This new group wanted everything put on more of a business-like footing. They wanted to exercise authority over the work of the Mission and send trustees to examine all the finances and properties and take control of them. Carey wrote; 'We have always thought ourselves masters of the funds produced by our own toil. We devote the whole to the cause of God, and wish to do so to our dying day. But the funds we produce have never been so merged into the Society's funds as to put them under others' control. We are your brothers, not your hired servants.' What the Society had invested in the Mission had been a trifling amount compared with what had been earned by hard work. The new committee had not known the Serampore missionaries personally. There was talk of the Society wanting to cut back on some of the work in Java and Ceylon. The idea of retrenchment was anathema to Carey who had always believed in expansion. There were rumours circulating that they were making private fortunes and feathering the nests of their sons. Nothing could have been further from the truth or more hurtful. Certainly John Marshman was proving himself exceedingly gifted and important to their work and an obvious successor. But their frugal life-style made all these accusations ridiculous.

The Society sent them five new missionaries who were warmly welcomed into the community and all was going so well. But sadly, they came with a hidden agenda and a critical spirit. Johns – one of the missionaries who was sent back home under Minto's orders - had spread poison against Marshman whom he felt had not tried hard enough to enable him to stay in India. Even Ryland (now Secretary in succession to Fuller) was affected. Friction grew, largely between the newcomers and Marshman. Carey knew accusations against his dear friend were utterly untrue and unfair. He could do none other than to staunchly stand by him. When Ryland had been led into criticism of Marshman, Carey wrote a terse letter telling him his letter to Marshman was insulting and unmerited. What he'd said was evil and he must acknowledge that and put it right with anyone whom he'd told. He ended it, 'I am your very affectionate but deeply wounded brother.' This all led to a sad and lengthy schism. The newcomers – including Carey's nephew Eustace - moved from Serampore to Calcutta, not to work in the Mission's Lall Bazar Union Church or the Mission's schools, but to set up their own ventures in an independent and competitive spirit. It seemed miraculous

That people in high places throughout the administration were begging the Serampore Mission to send missionaries to other places but the newcomers were not interested.

Carey in particular made every effort possible to bring about reconciliation with the young missionaries and urged meetings where they could talk things through and seek forgiveness from one another. This was largely achieved by the middle of 1820. But schism with the home society would last much longer. Ward, John Marshman, Hannah and Joshua himself each visited England during this period to try to put things right. Each failed. It was a long and protracted schism which seemed impossible to heal. Correspondence from the Society was cold and authoritarian.

The salaried young missionaries still occasionally stoked fires of resentment against the largely self-financing Serampore missionaries. Over a considerable period magazines and articles were written in Britain continually criticising the Serampore Mission and shamefully impugning their honour. 'Fake news' is not altogether a new phenomenon.

Eventually the Serampore Mission decided to divest themselves of all their properties and give them to British trustees, on condition that they could live there rent-free until their deaths. They had always intended for them to belong to the Society. This decision brought great relief to all and at last brought the painful schism to an end.

So many of the visionary ideas of the Serampore Mission would have failed to pass in a large London committee. Many of those ideas came from Carey but they arose from values shared by them all. There was consultation, mutuality, prayer and trust. They had been ably supported by people like Fuller, Sutcliff, and Ryland who knew them well and were 'of one heart and mind'. We can understand the Society wanting to look to the future and introduce safeguards, but their plans lacked respect for the achievements of the Serampore 'giants' who had spent their whole beings in service to God and the Indian people for a quarter of a century.

The difficult decade from 1820 to 1830 saw many other sad events: the death of Carey's much-loved Charlotte, of son Felix, of William Ward and John

Ryland, of Krishna Pal and the Marshman's eldest daughter, Susan, and of Ignatius Fernandez who had carried on Carey's work in the church in Dinajpur, founded in the indigo days. Furthermore, Carey suffered a bad fall which left him very disabled for many months. Marshman feared he would lose him too, but he battled on, having to be carried here and there and sitting to teach and to preach. His new wife Grace was a great help in nursing him back to health.

The next disaster was a flood which destroyed many homes, including Carey's own and he had to move into the college buildings. Probably even more painful from his point of view was the submerging of his garden in muddy water for a week with the loss of many plants. Repairs had to be made and the garden re-stocked. It was not possible to appeal to the home Society's committee for help. Carey added to his work-load the job of Bengali translatorship for the Government. This turned out to be very hard work and there was an 18 month backlog of work. He would declare that translating Ephesians was child's play compared with that of the involved legal documents with their impossibly lengthy sentences. But this job was to give him great joy in 1829 when at last sati was abolished by a determined Lord Bentinck and it was Carey's responsibility to translate the edict into Bengali. Carey didn't want an hour to be wasted before it was published.

Despite everything, the work of the Mission flourished with new workers, an increase in the number of mission stations and many conversions and baptisms.

'Come to terms quickly with your accuser.' Matthew 5:25

Q. How compatible are the modern business and management techniques employed by churches with vision and imagination?

Q. What place should authority have in the relationship between clergy and laity and between clergy and their structural 'superiors'; and in Baptist churches where does authority lie between ministers, diaconate and church meeting?

Q. How good is the Church at conflict resolution and reconciliation?

33

John Sutcliff
1752—1814

Andrew Fuller
1754—1815

John Ryland
1753—1825

8. Money

'Every wild animal of the forest is mine, the cattle on a thousand hills. I know all the birds of the air, and all that moves in the field is mine.'
Psalm 50:10,11

'The Lord shall fulfil all your need according to his riches in glory.'
Philippians 4:19

Carey was born into relative poverty. There would have been no question of his parents affording to pay for him to have an education, so he was very fortunate to have a charity school education. This was no preparation for university education and an apprenticeship was the best option available for him. We have seen him sinking into serious poverty in his early years of marriage and barely surviving as a young minister at Moulton, despite juggling three jobs. He even struggled at wealthier Leicester. It is indicative of how family finances were stretched that he was not on the list of donors to the newly-formed missionary society in 1792, although he did promise any proceeds from his *Enquiry*. (It is impossible to estimate his contribution for it was still being sold for BMS funds until a few years ago before it went out of print!) This makes it all the more remarkable that he could envision his denomination funding worldwide mission. He always intended that they should use Paul's tent-making as a model for working towards financial independence as soon as possible. But he developed a life-long belief that God would provide for their financial needs if it was his will they were doing. It was John Thomas' generous spirit that enabled them as a party of four adults, three children and a baby to travel to India, instead of the original plan of two adults and one child. He offered to go as a servant and persuaded Kitty to do so too. But in fact the Captain made generous provision for them all.

We know that Thomas' assurance of how cheap it would be to live in India and how easy to find suitable work proved woefully unrealistic. The money which was supposed to last a year was gone within about a month. His spendthrift ways left the whole family homeless, in painful and abject poverty. Dorothy and Kitty were by no means so sanguine as William, but he believed it was God who soon met their needs, initially with the dilapidated garden house in Manicktola, north of Calcutta, then by Charles Short's generous hospitality in Debhatta. William was resourceful and very hard working, but he was also sure it was God's provision when offered the well-paid job of indigo plantation manager that called them to Mudnabati. It was rather lonely there but much could be done with the money earned. A school was established, and a church. Then came the major expenditure of purchasing the indigo plantation at Kidurpur, not too far away. This was to prove an enormous financial loss when it became necessary to move to the Danish settlement at Serampore. How difficult this must have been for someone who had only recently got used to having money.

But compensations at Serampore were many, especially the community of missionaries, all of whom had skills that enabled them to earn money to build a remarkable mission base. There were homes for each family, communal areas for eating together, a worship centre (before the Danish Church was built by the Governor), boarding schools and printing works. Then came Carey's well-paid job at Fort William College which was to last for almost 30 years. The fact that none of them called their earnings their own and each had a frugal allowance for their needs meant that mission projects were abundantly funded and so much was accomplished. The income from the boarding schools brought in funding for free schools to be established for Bengali boys and later for Bengali girls. This included employing many people and funding largely Indian mission workers to set up far-flung mission stations which they hoped would become independent churches one day. The fact that the terrible fire of the Mission Press was calculated to have cost them a loss of nearly £10,000 shows just what a huge enterprise the Serampore Mission was. It was the faithful home supporters Fuller, Sutcliff, and Ryland in England and Christopher Anderson in Scotland, amongst others, who rallied British churches and other friends to supply their need so magnificently. The Serampore Mission gave God the glory. The fundraising really captured people's imagination and generosity. When Carey married the aristocratic Charlotte in 1808 she delighted in her beautiful house being rented out to fund the work of Indian evangelists. The wealth she brought to the marriage enabled Carey's family in England to receive much needed help. For some time they had all they needed to fund their ever-increasing vision.

One of their biggest and most expensive projects resulted from the desire to create Indian Christian scholars to grow the national church and evangelise India. Serampore College was built to a very high standard, funded by the Serampore community's enterprises as well as large contributions from friends in India, Britain and America-and even from the King of Denmark. It was intentionally accessible for poor as well as rich, for all castes and religions, with a very wide curriculum of Indian literature, philosophy and culture, western science and Christian Scriptures. Christian students, irrespective of denomination, were given free board and lodging in the Serampore community. Then there was the matter of salaried staff, but to start with Carey and his colleagues were its unsalaried lecturers.

All this happened during the difficult years after Fuller's death when the deteriorating relationship with new missionaries and with the home Society was moving towards schism. This makes the achievement all the more remarkable, but had they been relying on funding from the Society it would clearly never have happened. Many Christians in Britain and America made donations but stipulated they were to be spent on the theological education of Christians and were unhappy about the breadth of curriculum and the diversity of students. It was estimated that up to 1829 they had been able to contribute £68,000 from their acquired resources to the work of the Serampore Mission.

Felix proved financially needy during this period as he worked in Burma. He had sadly lost one wife and three years later married again. On a river journey returning from Serampore, the boat capsized and he lost both his wife and two young children. Also lost were a printing press he'd been given and a considerable sum of money. This had a very serious effect on his mental health. On a subsequent visit to Calcutta on behalf of the King, he lived far beyond his means, getting into debt and drinking heavily. Carey was not only embarrassed but had to find a way to settle his large debts personally. Felix feared to return to the king and spent three years roaming around before Ward happened to meet him and persuade him to return to Serampore. Fortunately he recovered and became very supportive to his father before dying from fever in 1820, only thirty seven years old.

Financial disaster was to affect the whole Calcutta area at the beginning of 1830 as one bank after another collapsed. Fort William College ceased its teaching and Carey was fortunate to be given a pension. The translatorship was suspended. Boarders at their school were unable to pay their fees. How could they pay the valued workers at their mission stations? How could Carey maintain his maintenance gifts to disabled sister Mary, Charlotte's sister in France and an orphan whose maintenance and education in England he was funding? All savings were lost. Friends in England did respond generously. People working in the mission stations also responded magnificently, agreeing to manage on less and to seek ways of maintaining themselves. Not one had to close. In all these difficult, distressing times, their faith in God remained unshakeable. 'I am convinced,' writes Carey to a friend, 'of God's infinite wisdom…God can raise us up help. It is his wont to make us realise our complete dependence on him.'

I know what it is to have little, and I know what it is to have plenty. In any and all circumstances I have learned the secret of being well-fed and going hungry, of having plenty and of being in need.'   Philippians 4:12-14

Q. Is money the most important thing we have to give?

Q. Have you experience of Christian activity failing because of too little or too much money invested in it?

Q. Christians in the UK and elsewhere gave very generously to the Serampore Mission. Why do you think this was?

9. Equality and humility

'...in humility regard others as better than yourselves.'
Philippians 2:3

William Carey was the son of a weaver and learned a working man's trade when he became a shoemaker and cobbler. There was little social mobility in that age, although in a sense his father did take a step up when he became teacher in the village school, the job his father had done before him. But you needed little qualification for a charity school beyond the respect of your community. William never forgot his humble roots and there were always those keen to remind him of them. Becoming a dissenter in his teenage years did nothing for his social status then. But being a Christian gave him a great sense of equality in the sight of God and that was all that mattered. It would form his life-long view that every individual was equally important to and loved by God whether slave in the West Indies or King of England, whether Dalit or Brahmin.

When living in Piddington and Hackleton he had become friends with John Newton, vicar of Olney, and William Cowper. In an earlier life Newton had been a ship's captain involved in the slave trade. No doubt they opened his eyes to the iniquities of this trade. Carey's sisters said they never heard him pray without praying for freedom for slaves. Maybe when in Moulton, but certainly in Leicester, Carey's family joined the sugar boycott. He met William Wilberforce and the Clapham Sect and Carey's fight against slavery became a life-long campaign. He lived long enough to see and rejoice in the abolition of the trade and eventual emancipation of the slaves in the West Indies. When in India there was an occasion when a young man working for the East India Company, W. Cunninghame, came to him one day to ask for his advice because he had inherited plantations in the West Indies.

'What do you think I should do?' he asked Carey.
'Don't you think you should go and free your slaves?' replied Carey.
And that is what he did.

We may look back on the French Revolution with horror, but especially in his time in Leicester, the ideas behind it were inspiring Christians like Carey, and others. Liberty, Equality, Fraternity: were they not Christian values? He mixed with republicans and was influenced by such people as Thomas Payne and his 'Rights of Man'. On one occasion Fuller reprimanded Carey when he refused to toast the King's health. Carey's belief in the equality of all in the sight of God followed him throughout life, making him deferential to all but also giving him the confidence to talk to and deal with anyone, irrespective of their social status. This meant that when eventually Indians were becoming Christians, he would insist that all who gathered at a communion service sat together as equals whatever their caste and whether Indian or European, rich or poor. The community came to realise in time, that this meant Christians of other denominations too should be able to share communion with them, whether or not they had been baptised as believers. (For some, back home, this was regarded as a step too far.)

Once when Carey was to preach in the Lall Bazar Chapel in Calcutta – in that poorest area of the city - he went into the pulpit to find a pair of leather sandals hanging inside. He immediately knew what they meant. Who did he think he was to hob-nob with Governor Generals, live in a fine house in Calcutta and be called 'Professor'? They knew he was just a common working man and a maker of leather shoes in England. Working with leather was the job of the lowest caste in India. He accepted the challenge: 'Yes, I am just a cobbler from England, and if God can use me, he can use all of us.'

Carey was clearly a man with considerable gifts but when he was called 'a genius' he strongly rebuffed the suggestion. 'No: I can plod,' he said. 'To that I owe everything.'

His humility meant he was always ready to consult others, listen to their advice and learn from them. This made him easy to work with and whatever he did was done collaboratively. When in 1800 he formed the mission community at Serampore, he may have been the *de facto* leader, but as far as he was concerned, all were equal. When they met for weekly meetings together to discuss community matters, it was assumed he would chair the meetings, but no, he insisted on people taking it in turns. I fear this almost certainly did not include the women! But it is clear Carey treated women too with great respect and so much of his work was for their liberation. He leaned heavily upon Hannah Marshman's skills, especially in pioneering education for girls. When Dorothy became very ill mentally and raged at William, many suggested he should put her in the Calcutta asylum or send her home, but he steadfastly resisted these suggestions. Hannah's son John who grew up in the Serampore community would later write of Carey, 'He always treated Dorothy with courtesy and compassion.'

As their work began to expand into other areas, a covenant was drawn up to be read three times a year at each mission station. It spoke of setting an infinite value on human souls, preaching Christ crucified and the nurture of personal religion. It spoke of recognising how minds worked and of possible cultural obstacles that should be avoided. They must always esteem and treat Indians as equals; cultivating their spiritual gifts and recognising that only Indians could win India for Christ. They must seek every opportunity for doing people good, giving without reserve and counting nothing they had as personal property.

As we have shown, the Serampore community itself was always having visitors. They were always glad to welcome missionaries of other denominations and offer them help and guidance based on their experience. One missionary to Burma, E. Pratchett, summed up Carey's servant leadership very well in a letter he wrote to a friend in 1811:

"(Carey) is most remarkable for his humility: he is a very superior man and appears to know nothing about it. The great man and the little child unite in him, and as far as I can see, he has attained to the happy art of ruling and overruling in connection with the others without his asserting his authority, or others feeling their subjection; and all is done without the least appearance of design on his part.'

Honours came Carey's way but seemed to affect him not at all! He was awarded an honorary doctorate in 1807 by Brown's University in America in recognition of his outstanding contribution to linguistic studies. He was eventually given the title of 'Professor of Bengali, Sanskrit and Marathi' at

Fort William College. Election as fellow of the Linnaean Society for his contribution to plant collection and classification was a very special honour, as was membership of the Asiatic Society and of Britain's Geological and Horticultural Societies, later to be called 'Royal'.

Towards the end of his life a visitor found him sitting as if in a trance. Eventually he interrupted him and asked what was on his mind.

'I know in whom I have believed, and am persuaded that he is able to keep that which I have committed unto him against that day. But,' continued the old man, 'when I think that I am about to appear in God's holy presence, and remember all my sins, I tremble.' He had wanted a simple funeral with no eulogy and to be buried in Charlotte's tomb with just the couplet from Isaac Watt's hymn on the side; 'A wretched, poor and helpless worm/ On thy kind arms I fall.'

When very near to death, Carey was visited by the missionary, Alexander Duff. Duff was respectfully listing all the achievements of Carey's distinguished missionary life. Carey whispered, 'Pray!'. Duff knelt and prayed and said goodbye. As he was going to the door, he thought he heard a feeble calling of his name. He went back and this is what Carey said: ' Mr Duff, you have been speaking about "Dr Carey, Dr Carey"; when I am gone, say nothing about Dr Carey, - speak about Dr Carey's Saviour.'

But speak of Dr Carey we do. Why? Because to talk about Carey *is* to talk about his Saviour. It is the story of a flawed human being, loved and forgiven by God, utterly committed to the will of God, whatever that should mean, whatever the cost. That *is* God's story. God could work great things because of Carey's commitment, because of his contagious faith, because of his humility, because he never gave up. His gifts were God-given and offered back to God. Carey would not really want to be singled out but would want us to remember all the important players in the story, in Britain, India, and America; Christians and others.

Humility is not thinking less of yourself, it's thinking of yourself less.'

- C.S. Lewis

Q. Jesus' ministry was particularly to the marginalised who enjoyed little social equality. How good is the Church today at embracing the same priority?

Q. How would we explain to Carey why we still tell his story?

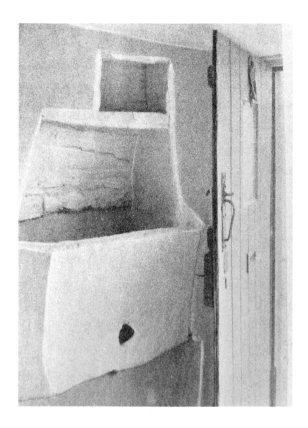

Trough for soaking leather in Carey's cobbler's cottage at Moulton.

10. Salvation and social action

'I came that they may have life and have it abundantly.' John 10:10

When John Ryland senior had called Carey 'an enthusiast', it was meant as a term of abuse, but clearly he was very enthusiastic about God's salvation. When he was converted in Hackleton, he was overwhelmed by the love and forgiveness of God which was deeply personal and demanded a response of love and commitment from him. He believed Jesus' death was God's way of showing the world how much he loved every single individual, and that included him. He wanted everyone to know it and experience the fulness of life of God's salvation. Evangelism mattered. But Carey and his colleagues knew that it was Indian Christians who would make the most effective evangelists to Indian people. Indeed it was not until seven years after arriving in India that Carey was able to rejoice in the first Indian convert, Krishna Pal. The newly formed community at Serampore witnessed his baptism together with that of Felix Carey at the end of the year 1800. This was the beginning of a breakthrough and the rapid growth of the indigenous Christian community. Krishna Pal himself became an enthusiastic missionary and saw many of his fellow countrymen become Christians. This was maximised by the strategic opening of more than a dozen mission stations manned by a mixture of European and Indian Christians, but mainly the latter.

But Carey's was no narrow going-to-heaven-when-you-die concept of salvation: it was particularly about this life, here and now. The more he had learned about the world and its problems the more aware he had become of the enormous need to share the Gospel. Slaves in the West Indies needed liberating. Captain Cook wrote of conflict and cannibalism in the South Sea islands. The French were ruled by a wealthy aristocracy who seemed to care nothing for the hunger and grinding poverty of the poor. How much they needed liberty, fraternity and equality! In Leicester he had become aware of the need for prison reform and better ways of treating the mentally ill. Salvation for Carey began with accepting Jesus as Lord. Carey was convinced this was the answer to the world's deepest needs and would lead to social justice and fulness of life. God's salvation was about justice and righteousness – putting things right, bringing order out of chaos here and now.

In India Carey was shocked by the expectation that women would sacrifice their babies – usually girls – to the river gods at festival times. These women and their babies were loved by God and needed saving. Vigorous campaigning based on the collection of shocking statistics led to the practice of infanticide being made illegal. Another social evil perpetrated against women was 'sati' – widow burning. When Carey first witnessed this he could hardly believe such horror, as a widow was led up to lie beside the body of her dead husband on his funeral pyre, and held down with branches as the fire was lit and the crowd made a great noise. There could be no second thoughts on the part of the widow. It was claimed that it was voluntary on her part and in accordance with their scriptures, but Carey had read their scriptures (and had translated much of them). He could argue that it was indeed mentioned in them but in no way commanded. Widows had no real place in Indian society, and sadly many were young women married to much older men. Sometimes men with more than one wife would leave more than one widow to die in this way. Campaigning for the abolition of sati took many years but the practice was eventually made illegal. In the Christian community remarriage of widows was encouraged.

People with leprosy were often ill-treated. Sometimes they were burned or buried alive. Belief in re-incarnation led to a belief that such people must have been wicked in a previous life and would stand a better chance in the next cycle of life. The Serampore Mission established medical centres and campaigned for more humane treatment of people with leprosy. A cure for leprosy would have to wait until the 20th Century. Setting up schools and lending libraries opened minds, enriched lives and undermined superstition; savings schemes tackled the problem of high interest rates for borrowers that exacerbated poverty.

Carey was fortunate to experience the benefits of education himself as a boy, even if only within the basic limitations of a village charity school. In

Hackleton, Moulton and Leicester he had tried his hand at teaching out of economic necessity, so it is not surprising that in India it had such a priority. The Serampore boarding schools for rich European children brought in a good income for the Mission as well as providing a Christian education. Places were much sought after and the reputation was high. But Carey's heart was particularly in the free schools for Bengali boys for whom paid-for education was not affordable, and it was especially in the education of girls for whom it was largely unheard of. His own teaching at Fort William College brought understanding and appreciation of Indian language and culture to civil servants, many of whom found or developed their Christian faith and became supporters of the Serampore Mission throughout their careers. But undoubtedly the most extraordinary and visionary educational enterprise was Serampore College, which celebrated its bicentenary in 2019. Many Christian converts came from the lower castes and had little or no education. If they and their children were to be effective Christian leaders and evangelists, they needed a well-rounded education. This would involve not only theology but arts and science subjects too, as well as an emphasis on Indian philosophy and literature. They would be taught in the medium of vernacular languages and would learn Sanskrit. Sanskrit had too long been the protected preserve of Brahmins, giving them alone access to sacred texts. This education would not be just for Christians. They needed to encounter difference and diversity. People would be able to attend from all over India. It was truly a university and enabled to confer degrees by the royal decree of the King of Denmark. Their charter was similar to that of Danish universities. Christian students were to be boarded free of charge and people of other faiths outside in more culturally appropriate accommodation. Much of the cost of this enterprise was borne by the Serampore Mission and its friends.

Even Carey's love of botany, horticulture, forestry and agriculture could point the way to food security and care of the environment.

Salvation is indeed multi-faceted. We have seen all these aspects forming goals of mission and development work ever since, but not usually master-minded-by one man and his community!

'What does the Lord require of you but to do justice, to love kindness and to walk humbly with your God?' – Micah 6:8

Q. How is the Church involved in the work of justice, liberation and mercy today?

Q Are there issues of need with society at home and abroad on which the Church is silent or just unaware?

Q Does the Church today show the same concern for Christian education as it does for secular education?

21st Century challenges

'History does not repeat itself but it does rhyme
attrib. to Mark Twain

In 2015 refugees were fleeing from Syria and surrounding countries in great numbers. It was disturbing to see unwelcoming attitudes towards these people despite their desperate circumstances. Leather footwear was worn out as mile after mile was covered. A group in Northampton decided to remake Carey's leather globe which had spoken so powerfully to him. They used it in 2016 to highlight and discuss the issues raised, taking it wherever they were invited. It is a globe made with different coloured leathers for different land masses, just like Carey's original, without borders or writing. It is an object of beauty made by a skilled craftsman in leather, with the aim of helping people reflect on the world as God sees it and loves it. (See back cover.) The question of refugees becomes increasingly challenging with the number of displaced persons in our world ever growing. Recently the number has been swelled by Afghan and Ukrainian refugees amongst many others.

Many of the challenges faced by Carey or presented to us by his life story remain the same today. There are still people in our world who have not encountered the Christian Gospel, and there are still people without access to the Bible in their own language. Slavery in the West Indies may be history, but it has left a legacy of discrimination and inequality. The 'Black Lives Matter' campaign has drawn attention to systemic racism throughout society and its institutions, shockingly even within the Christian Church. Slavery is still a many-headed monster, affecting for example workers in the sex industry or drug mules, people working for gang masters or in sweatshops, and those in bonded labour. We have failed to 'Make Poverty History'. After some success with The Jubilee Debt Campaign, the Covid 19 pandemic has left many of the poorest countries of the world in serious debt again. Girls are often denied an education and the 'Me too' campaign has highlighted domestic abuse and gender-based violence, especially against women.

Have attitudes towards other faiths changed? Carey first saw Hinduism as simply idolatrous and dangerous. His preaching emphasised its inadequacy in saving people, enabling forgiveness, or helping them with the problems of everyday life. Often those listening to his preaching would find commonality between their faith and his, but he was reluctant to recognise this. It seems this gradually changed to a more positive emphasis. He would tell them about Jesus dying for them to show them God's love and he expected this grace to melt their hearts. He learned how Hinduism affected every aspect of a person's life – socially, culturally, economically as well as religiously. Conversion to Christianity was something enormous and costly. When eventually this began to happen, those Indian Christians paid a huge price, becoming outlaws who had broken caste and become 'foreigners'. People were subjected to violence, lives were threatened, and lost, daughters seized for non-Christian marriage, houses burned, people were ostracised. It is clear that on a personal level, Hindus and Muslims were treated by the missionaries with great respect and courtesy. They were valued for their skills and abilities. They would all work happily together studying language, Bible translation and a myriad of other activities. Carey found like-minded people to campaign with against such social evils as sati. As he began to delve into Indian classic literature and sacred texts, he found wisdom and much to admire, and perhaps commonality too.

Differences of religious beliefs have always, it would seem, resulted in the most bloody of conflicts between major faiths and groups within those faiths. Christians have long been among both victims and perpetrators of persecution. Ecumenism took great strides forward in the 20th century: hopefully inter-faith dialogue will be accepted as a major challenge of the 21st. To share the Christian Gospel with people of another faith surely demands developing friendship and mutual understanding. We need to find common ground and affirm what is good. Shouldn't time and effort be invested in learning about that faith, and finding ways to work together for the common good? This is especially important in countries like the UK where such bridge-building is safe and non-threatening. Love, kindness, graciousness and an openness to difference should surely characterise Christian conduct. Confident delight in the Christian Gospel and admiration for the faith and insights of others are not incompatible but both call for humility.

Climate change is no doubt the biggest global challenge of our century. Carey believed science was the answer to superstition. Teach people astronomy and astrology would lose its power. Today we have people spreading 'fake news' and those who would deny climate change. The answer is the same. Carey believed that God loved the world in all its amazing variety. He worked tirelessly in areas of agriculture, horticulture and forestry to show how we must cherish the natural world, preserve its diversity, while using the generosity of its resources for the good of all.

Our world continues to suffer from war and conflicts, with weapons becoming ever more sophisticated and with all of us complicit in one way or another in our country's arms industry. (It funds our economic prosperity just as the Slave Trade did!) Our computer systems that have brought so much benefit to our lives have also brought the capacity for disastrous environmental problems like bitcoin mining and cybercrime.

What a catalogue of challenges! I'm sure you could add others. Carey responded to so many challenges in his day but not alone. His supporters at home were vitally important. He knew he could rely on their prayers, their money-raising in an emergency, and their advocacy both in the Church and wider society. His vision and Christian courtesy made him a leader whom his colleagues and supporters in India were happy to follow. His achievements were many but he saw them as the work of God that he was privileged to join in with.

"Blessed are those who hunger and thirst for righteousness, for they will be filled.' Matthew 5:6

A Final Challenge

Q. What are the dreams of God that the Church of today is invited to dream with him? Is our vision big enough, our commitment and obedience up to the job? How will we share the vision? How will we manage the time God has given us, and keep going when things are tough? What gifts, enthusiasms, interests, money could we offer to God? How can we work together with others? Do we have the humility of servant leadership?

Q. It's easy to recognise blind spots in 18th/19th Century Christians. Can we guess what future generations will think are those of ours?

Q. Where do we find prophets and visionaries today? (We need to look wider than the Christian Church.)

For more information or to plan a visit, visit www.thecareyexperience.co.uk

or email info@thecareyexperience.co.uk

or contact websites of the individual churches mentioned

Cover photographs by Jodie Dennis

Printed in Great Britain
by Amazon

41964162R00036